Matthew Perry the Undisclosed Biography

Childhood Abandonment and How it Affected His Fame and Fortune, Addiction and Journey Towards Recovery, Relationship Ups and Down to the Tragic End of a Friend

By Mark Morrison

Table of Contents

Disclaimer:

This book is an unofficial tribute book to Matthew Perry from a fan to support his legacy.

The information in this book is provided for educational and entertainment purposes only.

The information in this book has been compiled from reliable sources. It is accurate to the best of the author's knowledge; however, the author cannot guarantee its accuracy and validity and cannot be held liable for any errors or omissions.

If you use the information contained in this book, you agree that the author is free from and not liable for any damages, costs, and expenses, including any legal fees, potentially resulting from applying any of the information provided by this guide.

The disclaimer applies to any damages or injury caused by the use and application, whether directly or indirectly, of any advice or information presented, whether for breach of contract, tort, neglect, personal injury, criminal intent, or under any other cause of action. You agree to accept all risks of using the information presented inside this book.

If an individual uses this publication as the source of information, it does not imply that the author or publisher endorse the individual organization's knowledge. This book is an unofficial fan tribute and has not been approved or endorsed by Matthew Perry or his associates.

Chapter 1 - Echoes of Laughter: The Matthew Perry No One Knew

Beneath the luminescence of a stage light, a silence fell upon the set - a profound stillness that served as the counterpoint to the laughter Matthew Perry so effortlessly inspired. In these quiet moments, a stark contrast to the joviality he was famed for, the depth of his journey truly resonated. The humor that filled living rooms and etched itself into the zeitgeist was but the surface of a life rich with complexity and perseverance.

Grasping the essence of Matthew Perry's remarkable resilience and his journey to laughter begins by tracing the threads back to their origin. His story unfolds like a patchwork quilt, each piece a different home, a different chapter in the early narrative of a life destined to be anything but ordinary. Amidst the transience, a young Matthew found solace in the arts, a constant beacon that would eventually lead him to the warmth of the spotlight and the embrace of a global audience.

On a late summer's day, as the Berkshires stood witness, the quaint town of Williamstown, Massachusetts, welcomed Matthew Langford Perry into the world. His first cry on August 19, 1969, echoed against a backdrop of picturesque landscapes and the gentle undulations of this New England haven. With its verdant hills and historic charm, this serene setting was where the future star's journey commenced, marking the beginning of a life that would captivate audiences worldwide. It was here, nestled at the cusp of great natural beauty and the convergence of state lines, that Matthew's story unfolded, beginning with the union of John Bennett Perry and Suzanne Langford.

Yet, the idyllic setting belied the turbulence that would soon upend the Perry household. The marriage of his parents, a union barely a year old, began to unravel, leading to their separation before Matthew could even utter 'mom' or 'dad.' It was a fissure that marked the start of a nomadic existence that would challenge the young Perry to find constancy in change.

In those formative years, the silence of the night was often pierced by the cries of a baby seeking comfort. The remedy of the era, prescribed with well-meaning intent, was barbiturates, a solution that seems unfathomable now but was a common practice then. Little did they know that this early encounter with medication would foreshadow a theme that would recur throughout his life—a battle not with the shadows of the night but with the very means used to dispel them.

Matthew himself would later reflect on these nights with a poignant insight, pondering if the seeds of his later struggles were sown in those twilight hours when sleep was a chemically induced escape rather than a natural reprieve. It was a haunting thought, one that suggested his later sleep disturbances might be traced back to those earliest days when the developing brain was learning patterns it would carry into adulthood.

This chapter is not just a recounting of places and dates; it is the uncovering of a complex foundation laid down in Perry's youth—a foundation that would support a life of laughter, success, and the hidden battles that would test the very fabric of his being.

From Canadian Roots to Hollywood Beginnings

The landscape of Matthew Perry's youth was as varied and expansive as the nation of Canada itself, where he spent his childhood years. With each relocation—from Toronto's vibrant streets to Ottawa's stately calm and Montreal's cultural mosaic—Matthew's world grew, but so did a sense of isolation. Friendships were transient, much like the cities he called home. Yet, within these solitary stretches, a spark for performance and laughter began to kindle, setting the stage for the beloved humorist he would become.

Matthew's mother, Suzanne Langford, stood as a figure of quiet strength and achievement in this tableau. A beauty queen turned political aide, she worked alongside Pierre Trudeau, a charismatic leader who shaped the nation. In the halls of power, young Matthew glimpsed a world where poise and rhetoric held sway. Suzanne's remarriage to Keith Morrison, a name synonymous with television journalism, added another dimension to the young Perry's understanding of the public sphere.

Amidst the academic avenues of Rockcliffe Park Public School, nestled in Ottawa's green embrace, Matthew made a good friend—Justin Trudeau, who would also rise to national prominence. It was a friendship that bore the innocence of childhood yet was tinged with the foreshadowing of their respective futures. A lighthearted scuffle between the two boys, recounted years later with the silliness of hindsight, became a moment that resonated with fans, encapsulating Matthew's enduring charm.

Matthew's creative impulses simmered at Ashbury College. This all-boys school prized discipline and scholarship, a prelude to the burst of expression that would later define him.

When the time came to retrace his steps back to the United States at the tender age of fifteen, it was with a tapestry of experiences from his Canadian odyssey. The move to join his father in Los Angeles marked not just a change of address but the turning of a page to a new chapter. It was here, in the City of Angels, that Matthew's dreams would edge closer to reality in a land synonymous with stars and the stories they tell.

John Bennett Perry, Matthew's father, had made his mark in Hollywood, notably as the dapper sailor in the iconic Old Spice commercials of the 1970s and as a familiar face on the soap opera 'Falcon Crest' during the 1980s. Their paths diverged early when John and Langford parted ways in 1970, with John's acting ambitions taking him deeper into the industry, leading to a new family with Debbie Boyle in 1981.

Matthew's contact with his father was sporadic, mostly limited to Sunday phone calls—a distant yet admired figure who existed more on the screen and in print than in his day-to-day life.

Despite his admiration for his dad, Matthew yearned for a deeper connection and to piece together the puzzle of his paternal lineage that seemed as distant as the Hollywood sign.

During the rare visits to Los Angeles, the city of dreams and his father's domain, Matthew found himself amidst the buzz of showbiz. On one such visit, amidst the sets and the stage lights, he landed a minor role on the show '240-Robert', an opportunity that gave him a tantalizing taste of acting, sharing the screen with his father and the likes of Mark Harmon.

At the age of 15, Matthew faced a crossroads: to remain in the familiar backdrop of Canada or move to the United States to forge a bond with his father. It was a decision heavy with the weight of change but propelled by a desire to fill the gaps in his family narrative. In his heart, Matthew felt like an outsider in his own story, and moving to Los Angeles was a step towards finding where he truly belonged.

Matthew Perry's Fight with PM Justin Trudeau

Deciding Between the Court and the Stage

Matthew Perry found himself at a crossroads between two passions: the tennis court's thrill and the stage's allure. Tennis wasn't just a hobby for Matthew; he was so skilled that by age 13, he was already making waves in Canada's national rankings. He dreamt that moving to Los Angeles would bring him closer to his father and open doors to a possible future as a professional athlete.

Yet, there was another call that resonated deeply with Matthew—the call of the stage. His innate ability to draw laughter from those around him was undeniable. His wit and charm seemed to brighten any room effortlessly. At Ashbury College, he found his stride on stage in a major role in "The Death and Life of Sneaky Fitch," revealing his potential as a performer.

The decision to pivot fully into acting came when Matthew faced the stark reality of Los Angeles' fiercely competitive tennis scene. The players he encountered were of a different caliber, pushing him to acknowledge that his talents shone brighter under stage lights than on the tennis court.

Embracing his path as an actor, Matthew honed his craft at Buckley School in Sherman Oaks, taking his place among other aspirants of the performing arts. Further sharpening his skills, he attended classes at LA Connection, a well-regarded acting school that promised to be a forge for his burgeoning talent.

As high school days waned, Matthew began to find reconciliation with his past. Both his parents were present to celebrate his graduation—a symbolic moment that helped him appreciate the separate journeys that had brought his family to this point. The understanding dawned on him that perhaps the tapestry of his childhood, with all its unique threads, was meant to be as it was.

Amongst the figures in his life, Keith Morrison, his stepfather, stood out as a source of stability and camaraderie. A seasoned journalist, Morrison built his career at CTV, a major Canadian network, while Matthew was growing up in Canada. His career later led him to the Canadian Broadcasting Corporation. In a twist of serendipity, Morrison moved to Los Angeles in 1986 to join KNBC, NBC's television station in the city, and as fate would have it, Matthew's move to the States brought them geographically closer. The bond between stepfather and stepson was one of mutual respect and affection, a silver lining in the story of a boy navigating his path to manhood.

Breaking Into the Scene

Matthew Perry's journey into the heart of Hollywood was a steady ascent, each role building upon the last. It all started with his high school acting classes, which opened the doors to his initial television appearances. His first taste of the small screen came in 1985 with a guest appearance on the CBS sitcom 'Charles In

Charge.' This was Matthew's first step into the world of sitcoms, a genre where he would eventually shine brightly.

In 1986, he continued to build his portfolio with a role in 'Silver Spoons,' another popular sitcom that had shifted from NBC to reach a broader audience through syndication. These early roles gave Matthew a feel for the industry and a chance to showcase his budding talent.

Matthew's big break came in 1987 when he appeared on 'The Tracey Ullman Show,' a Fox network production known for its skits and comedy routines. The show is remembered for introducing 'The Simpsons,' which would become a television legend. Matthew's participation in such a ground breaking show marked a significant milestone in his early career.

1988 saw Matthew stepping into the world of film with 'A Night In the Life of Jimmy Reardon.' Although his role was brief and the film didn't create a significant stir at the box office or with critics, it represented a crucial moment for Matthew. Sharing the screen with River Phoenix, this film was an important learning experience and a stepping stone in the progression of his acting career.

First TV Appearance on Charles in Charge

His First Show

1987 marked the year Matthew Perry secured his first significant TV role on the fledgling Fox network's sitcom 'Second Chance.' The series presented a peculiar blend of comedy and supernatural themes, placing Matthew in the spotlight and leading to his first major hurdle in the acting world.

In 'Second Chance,' Matthew embodied Chazz Russell, a youthful incarnation of the central character Charles Russell, portrayed by Kiel Martin. The show's premise hinged on a quirky celestial judgment: Upon dying in 2011, Charles Russell finds himself in a cosmic limbo, not fit for heaven yet too benign for hell. His solution is to rewind time to 1987, guiding his younger self, Chazz, toward better life choices.

A memorable aspect of 'Second Chance' was the parallel lives of Charles and Chazz—Charles, now a convenience store owner, resided above the garage of his former house, entwining his present with his past. The dual portrayal by Martin and Perry often had them mirroring each other's style and movements, an inventive twist that showcased Matthew's burgeoning comedic talent, especially in physical humor.

After a nine-episode run, the show underwent a significant transformation, rebranded in 1988 as 'Boys Will Be Boys.' With the supernatural elements shelved and Martin's departure, the show's focus shifted to the earthly escapades of

Chazz and his friends. Matthew remained t the heart of the series, with his portrayal of Chazz still a highlight despite the changes.

Although 'Second Chance/Boys Will Be Boys' has faded from the mainstream memory, it remains a pivotal chapter in Matthew Perry's narrative. It was here, in the infancy of his career, that the seeds of his comedic genius were sown—seeds that would bloom resplendently in the years to come. Reflecting on those early days, Perry might have echoed the sentiment with a quip worthy of Chandler Bing himself: "Could there BE any more of a learning curve?" This blend of humor and heartfelt effort in his first substantial role laid the groundwork for a journey filled with laughter, challenges, and the indomitable spirit of a star in the making.

Thus, the curtain falls on Chapter One, leaving behind the echoes of a laugh track that would follow Matthew Perry from the nascent stage of his career to the peak of sitcom stardom.

Trailer of Matthew Perry's First Movie

Chapter 2 - Before Central Perk - Matthew's Rise to the Top

Matthew Perry's ascent in Hollywood was a testament to the reality that instant stardom is a rarity. Success in acting is often a product of time, dedication, and relentless perseverance. For Matthew, this path was marked by consistent effort and a steadfast commitment to his craft, even when the road to fame was anything but smooth.

The journey to establish himself as a household name required plenty of hard work and strategic choices. Navigating the entertainment industry required talent, a keen sense of direction, and an unwavering resolve. Despite his dedication, Matthew's path had many obstacles and uncertainties.

In the six years following the end of 'Second Chance/Boys Will Be Boys,' Matthew experienced a series of ups and downs. He managed to secure various roles, but many were minor parts that barely scratched the surface of his potential. His television appearances, while frequent, were often in roles that didn't quite stand out or lead to significant recognition.

During this time, Matthew made guest appearances in several well-known TV shows, including 'Just the Ten of Us,' 'Highway to Heaven,' 'Empty Nest,' and 'Who's the Boss?' These roles, albeit small, were crucial in keeping him visible in the industry and honing his skills, preparing him for the life-changing role that was just around the corner.

The year 1989 was a turning point for Matthew Perry as he began to carve a more noticeable niche for himself in Hollywood. His foray into popular television was marked by his appearances in three episodes of 'Growing Pains,' a beloved sitcom that allowed him a greater opportunity to showcase his comedic skills to a larger audience. This experience not only enhanced his visibility but also gave him valuable exposure to the world of mainstream sitcoms.

That same year, Matthew ventured into the realm of cinema with a role in 'She's Out of Control,' featuring alongside notable actors Tony Danza and Catherine Hicks. The film, however, didn't quite hit the mark with the movie-going public. It was met with lukewarm responses, one of which was from the iconic film critic Gene Siskel, who humorously commented that the film almost compelled him to give up his career in film criticism. This response, while disheartening, highlighted the unpredictable nature of audience reception in the entertainment industry.

In 1990, Matthew continued to expand his acting portfolio, this time transitioning to a biographical television film titled 'Call Me Anna,' which portrayed the life of the acclaimed actress Patty Duke. In this production, Matthew embraced the role of Desi Arnaz Jr., engaging with the complex layers of Duke's personal life, including her controversial and highly publicized relationship with Arnaz. This relationship stirred the public and media alike, partly due to the outspoken disapproval of Arnaz's mother, Lucille Ball. While the film delved into these intriguing aspects of Duke's life, it failed to secure a lasting place in the annals of memorable television films, echoing the brief and turbulent nature of Duke and Arnaz's real-life liaison.

This phase of Matthew's career, although peppered with significant opportunities, was characterized by brief and sometimes forgettable roles. His portrayal in 'Call Me Anna' was symbolic of the challenges he faced in these early years - capturing attention but not always leaving a lasting impact, reminiscent of Lucille Ball's challenges in pushing the boundaries on 'I Love Lucy.'

Despite these hurdles, Matthew's journey in Hollywood was marked by steadfast determination and resilience. He understood that endurance and a continuous commitment to his craft were essential in the unpredictable world of acting. This perseverance soon led him to another significant opportunity on television. It paved the way toward the iconic role that would eventually catapult him to stardom, signifying his arrival as a major player in television comedy.

Taking Another Shot with 'Sydney'

In his relentless pursuit of an acting career, Matthew Perry took another significant step in 1990 by securing a role in the CBS sitcom 'Sydney.' Understanding the often lengthy and uncertain path to success in Hollywood, Matthew was prepared for the rigorous journey ahead.

'Sydney' presented Matthew with a substantial opportunity. He starred alongside Valerie Bertinelli, playing the role of Billy Kells, the brother of the titular character Sydney Kells. The plot revolves around Sydney's move from the bustling streets of New York to her quieter hometown, where she sets up a private detective agency. Billy, portrayed as a keen yet inexperienced police officer, aims to help his sister navigate her new life in this smaller community.

The show was anticipated to be a hit, especially considering it was Bertinelli's first significant role on CBS since the beloved 'One Day At a Time.' To create a buzz, 'Sydney' even featured an appearance by Pat Harrington Jr., a nod to Bertinelli's past success. However, despite these promising elements and considerable efforts from the cast and network, the sitcom failed to capture the audience's attention. After a run of just thirteen episodes, 'Sydney' was cancelled. Its remaining episodes were quietly aired during the summer, traditionally associated with lower TV viewership.

Amidst the professional dynamics of 'Sydney,' Matthew, who was just 19 then, developed a youthful infatuation with the 30-year-old Bertinelli. He playfully dreamed of a romantic connection, even though she was married to Eddie Van Halen, the renowned rock musician. This backstage crush led to a memorable, albeit unanticipated, moment where Matthew and Valerie shared an extended kiss, while Eddie Van Halen was present but unaware, having dozed off. Despite the innocent flirtation and close working relationship, Matthew and Valerie's connection remained firmly in the realm of friendship, a testament to their professionalism and mutual respect.

This period of Matthew's career, marked by his involvement in 'Sydney,' was not just another step in his professional journey but also a time of personal exploration and understanding of the delicate balance between dreams and reality in acting.

Finding His Stride in 'Home Free'

In 1993, Matthew Perry was ready to take on a new challenge in the world of television with the ABC sitcom 'Home Free.' Stepping into the leading role, Matthew found himself at the center of a show that promised potential, backed by a team of notable names both in front of and behind the camera.

'Home Free' allowed Matthew to work in a production buzzing with talent. The show was co-created by the accomplished sitcom writer Tim O'Donnell, known for his successful forays into television comedy. The cast included seasoned sitcom actress Marian Mercer, 'Soap' star Diana Canova, and Dan Schneider, who would later gain fame as a producer of children's television. Adding to this ensemble was Alan Oppenheimer, the iconic voice of Skeletor, ensuring a diverse range of acting experience and style. The show also boasted a theme song by Christopher Cross and a score by Mark Mothersbaugh from Devo, adding a musical flair to its creative arsenal.

In 'Home Free,' Matthew portrayed Matt Bailey, a young, carefree freelance journalist enjoying life under the same roof as his mother, Grace (played by Mercer). Matt's laid-back lifestyle shifts when his sister Vanessa (Canova), along with her two children from a previous marriage, moves back into their family home. This new living arrangement prompts Matt to re-evaluate his carefree approach to life.

The show allowed Matthew to further showcase his comedic abilities, with much of the storyline revolving around Matt's attempts to adopt a more responsible demeanor, especially in setting a positive example for Vanessa's children. His journey toward maturity was humorously juxtaposed with his professional life, where his friend (played by Schneider) and boss (Oppenheimer) often added to his challenges.

Despite the talents assembled and its promise, 'Home Free' faced the harsh realities of television ratings. After airing just five episodes in early 1993, the show got cancelled due to low viewership. The remaining eight episodes were relegated to the less coveted summer slot on ABC's 'TGIF' line-up—a stark contrast to the fanfare typically associated with this prime-time block during the regular season. The summer airings, with minimal promotion, did little to salvage the show, leading to its cancellation.

For Matthew, 'Home Free' was another step in his evolving career—a journey marked by highs and lows, learning and growing with each role. This experience, though short-lived, was instrumental in shaping his approach to acting and understanding of the unpredictable nature of television success.

Another Attempt at Stardom with 'LAX 2194'

Undeterred by the industry's challenges, Matthew Perry continued his quest for the perfect role in 1994, landing parts in two new pilot episodes. The first of these was an ambitious comedy titled 'LAX 2194.'

Pilot episodes are a unique breed in television. They serve as the initial window into what a show might become, sometimes evolving into a beloved series, while others undergo significant transformations before reaching the audience. Some pilots, however, don't make it past their initial airing, ending up as one-off TV specials or are shelved and forgotten.

In the vast world of television, many pilots fade into obscurity, like 'Heat Vision and Jack,' 'Lookwell,' or the attempt to adapt the 'Bubsy' video game into an animated series. 'LAX 2194' unfortunately fell into this category, a pilot that quickly vanished from the public consciousness. But what set it apart was its indirect link to a future success story, a detail that would later become a curious footnote in Matthew's career.

The premise of 'LAX 2194' was set far in the future, with the plot revolving around the comedic antics of baggage handlers at Los Angeles International Airport in the year 2194. These handlers dealt with an eclectic mix of aliens, interstellar travelers, and various futuristic challenges, creating a humorous, albeit chaotic, vision of the future. The concept was certainly unique, but the question remained: would this science fiction comedy find its place in a genre where many shows are often remembered more for their quirks than their quality, such as 'ALF,' 'Out of This World,' or 'Small Wonder'?

The hopeful beginnings of 'LAX 2194' did not translate into a successful launch. Despite the combined talents of Matthew Perry, actress Kelly Hu, and improv comedy star Ryan Stiles, the show's premise failed to capture the interest of network executives. In the competitive arena of television, where new concepts battle for attention, 'LAX 2194' was left behind as networks prioritized other projects. It was a disappointment but not an unusual fate in the unpredictable world of pilot episodes.

As 'LAX 2194' quietly receded from the horizon, another opportunity was rapidly approaching. The creators of an upcoming show had set their sights on Matthew, impressed by his talent and charisma. When they learned that 'LAX 2194' wouldn't be moving forward, they saw their chance to bring Matthew on board for their own project.

This new opportunity was poised to become not just a successful TV show but one of the most iconic and beloved series in television history. For Matthew Perry, this was more than just another role—it was the gateway to unprecedented fame and the pivotal moment of his acting career. He was on the verge of becoming a household name, a face recognized in living rooms around the world.

However, the glittering allure of fame often comes with its own set of challenges. As we turn the page to the next chapter in Matthew Perry's story, we'll explore the complex interplay of success and personal struggle. His journey through the highs of stardom combined with the need to maintain his well-being and sobriety. The next chapter will delve into how, amidst the laughter and applause, Matthew navigated the intricate path of balancing his skyrocketing career with his personal life.

Matthew Perry on LAX 2194 Unsold TV Pilot

Chapter 3 - The Start of a New Era - the Beginning of Friends

Every iconic TV show has its genesis, a unique story of how it came into being. Consider 'The Simpsons,' which originated from a segment on 'The Tracey Ullman Show.' Or 'Laverne and Shirley,' born as a spin-off from 'Happy Days,' which itself first appeared in an episode of 'Love American Style.' Then there's 'MASH,' which transitioned from a Robert Altman film based on Richard Hooker's novel.

So, what about 'Friends'? Its beginnings may not have the dramatic backstory of these other series, but its journey to the screen was a culmination of years of creative development. For Matthew Perry, it represented the culmination of years of hard work and perseverance in the industry—a significant turning point just on the horizon.

'Friends,' unlike some of its predecessors, wasn't spun off from an existing show or adapted from a different medium. Instead, it was a fresh concept, carefully crafted and honed over time. Its conception was less about spin-offs or adaptations and more about capturing the essence of an era and the relatable experiences of young adults. For Matthew, joining the cast of 'Friends' was about to mark the beginning of an exciting new chapter that would catapult him into a new realm of stardom and success.

David Crane and Marta Kauffman, seasoned television writers, had already made their mark on the TV landscape with various projects. In 1990, they ventured into new territory with the creation of 'Dream On' for HBO. This show was a bold exploration of the freedoms offered by premium cable television, unafraid to push boundaries with its explicit content, including nudity and uncensored language. 'Dream On' stood out for its daring approach, leveraging the liberties of being on a subscription-based network.

Despite their success in the cable TV sphere, Crane and Kauffman were looking to expand their horizons. They aspired to bring their creative flair to network television's broader and more diverse audience. However, this move meant adapting to a different set of rules — network TV came with its limitations and censorship guidelines, a stark contrast to the creative freedom they enjoyed at HBO.

Moreover, transitioning to network television presented an exciting opportunity to work with a wider array of talent. The mainstream network environment promised access to a larger talent pool, including big names in the industry. For Crane and Kauffman, this was a chance to showcase their storytelling abilities on a grander scale, reaching a wider audience while navigating the unique challenges of network TV production.

So, Dave and Marta, armed with their experiences and insights from cable TV, set out to create a television show with a fresh perspective — one centered on the lives of twenty-somethings navigating the complexities of city life. This age, brimming with uncertainty and exploration, had rarely been the sole focus of a TV show. It's a period of transition where adulthood has just begun, yet the path of life isn't fully charted. The idea was to capture the essence of this liberating, albeit daunting, phase where one's identity and future are still taking shape.

In 1993, they presented their idea to Warren Littlefield, the then-president of NBC. Littlefield was scouting for a show that emphasized the importance of friendships. He believed that the concept of the traditional family, a staple of many TV shows, was evolving. People were increasingly valuing friendships, sometimes even more than romantic relationships. This shift in social dynamics resonated with Littlefield, who saw potential in a show that mirrored these contemporary trends.

The concept for the show was further inspired by Dave and Marta's own life experiences. Having lived in a complex surrounded by diverse individuals, they drew from these interactions to formulate the idea of six friends sharing their lives in the bustling city of New York.

The show that would eventually become 'Friends' initially started as 'Insomnia Café.' It underwent several title changes before the creators settled on the simple yet evocative title of 'Friends.' But how Matthew Perry landed his career-defining role on this show is as fascinating as the show's evolution.

Matthew's initial connection with creators David Crane and Marta Kauffman came when he guest-starred in an episode of 'Dream On' in 1992. This early collaboration set the stage for what was to come. However, his path to 'Friends' was nearly derailed by his involvement in 'LAX 2194.' As he was committed to this pilot, it seemed for a time that he might miss out on the opportunity to be part of 'Friends.'

But destiny had other plans. Once 'LAX 2194' was not picked up, Matthew became available for the 'Friends' pilot. Crane and Kauffman had already recognized Matthew's exceptional talent. They saw in him an actor who could bring their script to life, making even the most challenging dialogues sparkle with humor and authenticity. They were looking for his ability to infuse even underdeveloped jokes with vibrancy and energy.

This stroke of luck, combined with Matthew's undeniable charisma and dedication, led Crane and Kauffman to cast him in 'Friends.' As it turned out, the decision to not move forward with 'LAX 2194' was a fortunate turn of events for the 'Friends' team. It opened the door for Matthew to step into what would become not just a role but a defining part of his career and the landscape of 90s television culture.

Matthew Perry on Dream On: One of the first original shows on HBO to really take off

Matthew's Big Break

The long-awaited breakthrough in Matthew's acting career came with his casting in 'Friends.' He brought Chandler Muriel Bing to life, a character with a unique blend of sarcasm, wit, and vulnerability. This role was poised to define Matthew's career and leave a lasting impact on sitcom history.

Chandler Bing quickly became one of the show's standout characters. Chandler was known for his sharp humor and awkward charm, and his backstory added depth and complexity to his character. He was the son of an extravagantly dressed burlesque performer and a writer of erotic novels. This family dynamic played into the show's narrative in both humorous and poignant ways. Throughout the series, there were subtle insinuations about Chandler's sexuality, hinting at the possibility of him being gay, though the show portrayed him as straight.

This aspect of Chandler's character led to initial confusion among the cast. Lisa Kudrow, who brilliantly portrayed the eccentric Phoebe Buffay, admitted that upon her first reading of the script, she had the impression that Chandler would be a gay character. This ambiguity and the humor it generated contributed to the show's dynamic and the depth of its characters, making 'Friends' a nuanced and progressive show for its time.

Part of Chandler's character development in 'Friends' drew inspiration from Matthew's personal life. Like Chandler,

Matthew experienced the impact of his parents' divorce during his formative years. This significant event in Chandler's backstory led to prolonged periods of denial and personal struggle, mirroring Matthew's own experiences. For Chandler, these struggles manifested in behaviors like bed-wetting, a sensitive portrayal of the challenges he faced during his youth.

Additionally, Chandler's interactions with women were complex and often marked by difficulty expressing his feelings, a trait Matthew could relate to. This added an element of authenticity to Chandler's attempts at navigating relationships throughout the series.

A distinctive aspect of Chandler's character was his unique speech patterns, something viewers found relatable. His tendency to accentuate the wrong parts of sentences reflected the real-life difficulty many people face in verbal expression. As the series progressed, Chandler, and by extension Matthew, demonstrated a conscious effort to refine his speech, showing a character growth parallel to the show's development.

Chandler's humor, often seen through his penchant for making jokes and posing rhetorical questions, served as a defense mechanism. This showed through in his humorous self-description, where he quipped that his surname 'Bing' translates to 'the turkey is done' in an imaginary language. Other characters often acknowledged this humor, and advised him to embrace his comedic nature as his unique strength. Chandler himself encapsulated his quirky humor with remarks like, "I say more dumb things in the morning than anyone says all day long."

Chandler's career as an executive and processing manager in 'Friends' was a significant aspect of his character, reflecting the job dissatisfaction common among many in their twenties and thirties. Despite the high salary, Chandler's discontent with his job resonated with viewers who found themselves in similar situations — well-compensated but unfulfilled. This theme was explored further in the series when Chandler decided to leave his lucrative position for a junior copywriting job that, while paying less, brought him more happiness.

The relationships Chandler had with the other characters were central to the show. His college friendship with Ross Geller (played by David Schwimmer) was a cornerstone of his backstory. Through Ross, he became acquainted with Ross's sisters, Monica Geller and Rachel Greene (played by Courteney Cox and Jennifer Aniston, respectively). Completing the group were Phoebe Buffay and Joey Tribbiani, played by Lisa Kudrow and Matt LeBlanc. The dynamics and interactions among these six friends formed the heart of 'Friends,' endearing them to audiences worldwide.

The show also delved into Chandler's financial status, highlighting how he was the most financially secure member of the group. His approach to money management and the decision to save for life after marriage, rather than indulging in an extravagant wedding, was another storyline that viewers found appealing. It underscored Chandler's pragmatic and responsible side, even as he navigated the complexities of friendships and romantic relationships on the show.

The theme of coping with embarrassment was a significant facet of Matthew's character in 'Friends.' The universal dread of humiliation resonated strongly with audiences as they watched him navigate through cringe-worthy scenarios with a blend of humor and desperation. His elaborate lengths to avoid uncomfortable truths, like the absurd escape to Yemen to sidestep a breakup, were moments that highlighted his unique comedic approach to life's awkward situations.

Matthew's portrayal of a man navigating the complexities of relationships added another layer to his character. Despite various romantic escapades, including unexpected kisses with Rachel, Phoebe, and even Joey, his deep-seated feelings for Monica remained a constant thread. Their friendship blossomed into a meaningful relationship, eventually leading to marriage. This steady and evolving romance sets him apart from the other characters, showcasing a commitment to a deeper, more enduring connection.

As the series unfolded, more serious themes were woven into his storyline, particularly around the idea of starting a family. He and Monica faced the challenging reality of infertility, a sensitive subject that the show approached with care and authenticity. Their decision to adopt, culminating in the joyous surprise of adopting twins in the series finale, was a poignant conclusion to their journey. This storyline explored the emotional complexities of infertility and adoption and reinforced the enduring themes of love and family that were central to 'Friends.'

Chandler was Worth Plenty of Laughs in Every Episode

From Struggle to Stardom with Friends

As 'Friends' progressed through its ten-year run, Matthew Perry found himself in a whirlwind of success. His relationship with the rest of the cast wasn't just professional; they became close friends. This strong bond led them to renegotiate their contracts, a testament to their unity. Their efforts paid off remarkably, with each actor eventually earning $1 million per episode, a rare feat in television history.

The show itself, spanning from 1994 to 2004, became a cultural phenomenon, with Matthew appearing in every single one of the 236 episodes. The series finale drew in over 50 million viewers, placing it among the most-watched TV events ever. This level of success was something few shows have ever achieved.

For Matthew, being part of 'Friends' meant more than professional success. It was a period where he felt a genuine sense of belonging, a contrast to the earlier years of his life where finding acceptance and appreciation had often been a struggle. The show provided a stable, supportive environment that he had longed for.

However, with this newfound fame came its own set of challenges. Navigating the highs of success while maintaining personal stability was not easy. Despite the laughter and camaraderie on screen, Matthew faced his own battles off-screen. As we close this chapter on Matthew's rise with 'Friends,' it's clear that his journey was a complex mix of personal and professional triumphs and trials, reflecting the often-turbulent nature of life in the entertainment industry.

Chapter 4 - A Burgeoning Film Career and New Drug Struggles

The eternal debate between pursuing a career in television versus film is an intriguing one. On one hand, a career in film carries the allure of high-stakes excitement. The cinematic world, often involving multi-million dollar projects, has the power to leave an indelible mark on cultural landscapes. The glamour of film, with its grand parties and luxurious work trailers, is undeniably appealing. Moreover, forging lasting connections with influential filmmakers and industry executives is a common perk of the movie business.

On the other hand, a television career offers unique rewards. A successful TV role can provide stability and longevity, a rarity in the often transient acting world. The longevity of a show like 'The Simpsons,' which has captivated audiences for over three decades, is a testament to television's enduring appeal and financial viability. Its cast members, enjoying both fame and financial security, demonstrate the potential of a successful TV career.

For Matthew Perry, his role in 'Friends' was a golden ticket to success, comparable to the achievements of the 'Simpsons' cast. Earning over a million dollars per episode, his role on the show wasn't just financially rewarding; it showcased his innate charm and comedic talent. 'Friends' played a crucial role in sustaining NBC's popularity in the post-'Seinfeld' era, holding its own even amidst the rise of reality TV and ABC's 'Who Wants To Be a Millionaire.'

The show's success also opened doors for its cast members in the film industry. The off-seasons of 'Friends' provided ample opportunities for the actors to explore cinematic roles. Matthew Perry and his co-stars leveraged this time to delve into various film projects, broadening their horizons beyond the small screen. This flexibility to oscillate between television and film is a luxury afforded by the show's success and schedule, allowing them to enjoy the best of both worlds.

Matthew's journey through 'Friends' not only cemented his status as a television icon but also paved the way for his foray into the film industry, exemplifying the diverse paths an actor can navigate in entertainment.

When Chandler Met Julia

In the mid-90s, Matthew Perry found himself in the spotlight for his role in 'Friends' and his personal life. In 1995, he had a brief but notable relationship with Julia Roberts, one of the biggest film stars of the time. Julia, renowned for her roles in 'Pretty Woman,' 'Hook,' 'The Pelican Brief,' and 'Something To Talk About,' was at the peak of her career. Meanwhile, Matthew was making waves on television with 'Friends.' A relationship between two such prominent figures in the entertainment industry naturally garnered significant attention.

However, the romance between Matthew and Julia was short-lived. Despite a strong friendship foundation, they both recognized that the pressures and demands of their respective careers could potentially hinder their relationship. An interesting development during their time together was Julia's guest appearance on an episode of 'Friends.' This episode, masterminded by Marta Kauffman, aired right after the Super Bowl in 1996 and was a major success, drawing over 50 million viewers.

The split between Matthew and Julia happened soon after this high-profile episode. Matthew's feelings of inadequacy in the relationship played a role in their breakup. He held Julia in high esteem and worried that he couldn't match her stature in the industry. The thought of potentially losing her in a long-term relationship was a prospect Matthew found too daunting to face.

This brief romantic chapter in his life was a mix of professional triumph and personal introspection, reflecting the complexities of dating in the limelight.

Matthew's Box Office Charm in 'Fools Rush In'

Although he had starred in a few different films before hitting it big, Matthew finally got some lead roles in major productions, and not just TV-movies or things culled from failed pilots. His journey in film took a significant turn in 1997 with the romantic comedy 'Fools Rush In.' In this movie, he stepped away from his television persona to embrace the lead role of Alex Whitman, a project manager who experiences a life-changing one-night stand in Las Vegas. This fleeting encounter leads to unexpected consequences when he discovers that the woman he was with is pregnant. The film navigates the complexities of his newfound attachment to her and the tough choices he faces between his burgeoning romance in Las Vegas and his thriving career in New York.

Co-starring with Salma Hayek, 'Fools Rush In' enjoyed moderate success at the box office, grossing $42 million against a budget of $20 million. While the film received a mixed reception from critics, it highlighted Matthew's box office appeal. Renowned critic Roger Ebert, known for his discerning reviews, praised Perry and Hayek's performances. This role marked a significant milestone for Matthew, showcasing his ability to carry a film and connect with audiences in a leading role outside his established television success.

This Film Proved to be a Huge Hit

Matthew's First Adult Drug Struggle

An early, unintended brush with drugs in Matthew Perry's life involved barbiturates, administered by his parents to aid his sleep during toddlerhood. This early experience unknowingly set a precedent for later struggles with substance use. The pivotal moment came while filming 'Fools Rush In,' when an on-set injury pushed him towards substance use as a form of self-medication. What initially seemed like a solution to his problems soon revealed itself as a path to further complications.

The roots of his challenges with addiction traced back to his teenage years, beginning a pattern that would extend into his adult life. At fourteen, he embarked on a journey with alcohol, starting innocuously with beer and escalating to harder substances like Andres Baby Duck wine and, eventually, quarts of vodka. This progression from casual drinking to more severe forms of alcohol consumption marked the early stages of a long-term battle with addiction.

As he navigated the complexities of his burgeoning career, Matthew found himself turning to prescription painkillers. Medications like Vicodin, OxyContin, and Xanax, initially sought for relief, gradually became elements of a larger, more daunting struggle. His experience with these substances was a tangle of seeking comfort while simultaneously confronting their growing influence over his life. This ongoing battle with addiction was not just a personal struggle but one that would eventually intertwine with his professional journey, presenting challenges and learning experiences along the way.

On the set of 'Fools Rush In,' a jet-skiing mishap caused a significant injury for Matthew Perry. This accident became the catalyst for his dependency on Vicodin, a medication he initially turned to for pain relief. Vicodin, known for its potent analgesic properties, combines hydrocodone and acetaminophen. However, its effectiveness in alleviating pain comes with a high risk of addiction and severe health implications.

The use of Vicodin, especially in the entertainment industry, is often a double-edged sword. While it offers temporary relief, the drug's opioid nature makes it highly addictive and dangerous. Excessive consumption can lead to severe respiratory issues, and its interaction with alcohol is particularly hazardous, potentially leading to life-threatening situations. Despite these risks, the immediate relief it provides from physical pain makes it a tempting choice for many, including Matthew, at that time. His continued use of Vicodin, despite its dangers, was a testament to the intense discomfort he was trying to mitigate. This period marked a challenging phase in Matthew's life, where the urgency to alleviate pain clashed with the perils of dependency on a powerful prescription drug.

Matthew Perry's approach to socializing was atypical for someone in his position. Unlike many celebrities, he wasn't attracted to parties or large social gatherings. Instead, he found solace in quieter activities, like taking Vicodin and watching movies. This routine, though seemingly harmless, involved consuming up to five pills at a time, a clear indicator of the seriousness of his dependence.

Despite his increasing reliance on Vicodin, Matthew maintained certain boundaries. He was acutely aware of the dangers of mixing the drug with alcohol and steered clear of this hazardous combination. Furthermore, he set limits on the types of substances he would use. Heroin, for instance, was a line he was not willing to cross, showing a level of caution even amidst his growing drug use.

Matthew's struggle with drug use was a private battle, one he adeptly concealed from the public eye. He was fully aware of the potential for judgment and scrutiny from others if his drug use became known. This awareness fueled his discretion as he navigated the challenging waters of maintaining his public persona while dealing with his issues. His willingness to take such risks highlighted the complexity of his situation, caught between the need for relief and the pressures of public life. The dichotomy of Matthew's public success and private struggles painted a picture of a man grappling with the realities of fame and addiction; a battle often fought far from the spotlight.

Besides his quiet battle with addiction, Matthew's struggles intensified during his time on 'Friends.' Even as the show soared in popularity, he was dealing with a dependency on painkillers behind the scenes. This internal battle contrasted sharply with his onscreen persona, leading to several rehab stints. It wasn't until the ninth season, a phase marked by sobriety, that Matthew's full potential as an actor shone through, earning him an Emmy nomination.

The depth of his addiction became more apparent around the sixth and seventh seasons. Jennifer Aniston's confrontation about alcohol odor was a jarring moment that pierced through his veil of secrecy. Realizing his condition was becoming perceptible to those around him, Matthew knew it was time to seek serious help. His decision to enter rehab was pivotal, signifying his commitment to his health, career, and relationships with his colleagues.

In rehab, Matthew faced the arduous journey of overcoming his addiction, a challenge compounded by the pressures of his public life. This step towards recovery was critical in maintaining his role in 'Friends' and preserving the relationships he had formed with the cast and crew. His struggle and subsequent effort to get clean were not just about personal redemption but also about upholding his professional responsibilities and commitment to one of television's most beloved shows.

As Matthew continued navigating his recovery journey, a particularly heart-wrenching moment unfolded parallel to a significant event on 'Friends.' The seventh season featured the long-awaited wedding of Chandler and Monica, a high point for both the show and Matthew's character. Yet, as this iconic scene marked a celebratory moment on screen, Matthew's reality off-screen was starkly different. After filming the wedding episode, he immediately went back to a detox center, escorted by a sober companion from the set. This moment was laden with emotional conflict for Matthew, feeling a sense of letting down those around him while struggling to maintain the façade of his character amidst his personal battles.

This challenging period reflected the complexities Matthew faced during his time on 'Friends.' The show's success was a professional triumph, with fans eagerly following the lives of Chandler and his friends in New York. 'Friends' had become a staple of broadcast television and a beloved long-running series. Alongside this, Matthew's burgeoning career in film was taking shape, promising new avenues for his talents.

Despite the acclaim and opportunities, Matthew's personal journey was fraught with challenges. Balancing his role in one of television's most popular shows with the efforts to overcome his addiction was an ongoing struggle, marking a period where personal trials shadowed his professional achievements. As he grappled with these issues, Matthew's journey on 'Friends' continued to be a tale of contrasting experiences – immense success in the backdrop of a personal quest for healing and stability.

As we revisit Matthew Perry's journey, it's important to recall that his initial and seemingly innocuous encounter with barbiturates during childhood was part of a larger, more complex narrative of substance abuse. This early experience, set in motion by his parents to address sleep difficulties, unknowingly foreshadowed his later struggles with addiction. It's a poignant reminder of how early influences can unknowingly shape one's future. In the world of fame and fortune, the allure and accessibility of drugs can be overwhelming, leading even the most successful individuals down a difficult path. The pressure to use drugs can come from various sources, while others might turn to them out of a sense of isolation or as a coping mechanism for the challenges of celebrity life. The impact of drug addiction is a narrative all too common in Hollywood, affecting countless stars across generations. The stories of Judy Garland, who tragically succumbed to a barbiturate overdose, and River Phoenix, whose life ended abruptly due to a heroin overdose, are stark reminders of the devastating consequences of substance abuse. Their tales are echoed in the struggles of many other celebrities who grappled with addiction amidst their fame. Yet, there are also stories of hope and recovery. Jamie Lee Curtis and Elton John are notable examples of stars who successfully overcame their addiction, emerging stronger and continuing their careers with renewed vigor. Their journeys of sobriety offer a beacon of hope, a testament to the possibility of overcoming addiction and reclaiming one's life. As we conclude this chapter, the narrative of Matthew Perry finds itself at a crossroads. His battle with sobriety, set against the backdrop of his escalating fame, presents a dichotomy of success and personal struggle. The question lingers: will Matthew find a path to recovery akin to Jamie Lee

Curtis and Elton John, or will he face the darker outcomes that befell Judy Garland and River Phoenix? The next chapter in Matthew's story will delve deeper into his foray into the film industry, exploring how his ongoing battle with addiction added layers of complexity to his professional endeavors and personal life.

Chapter 5 - Further Movie Stardom

In the unpredictable world of filmmaking, not every project is successful, a reality that even the most esteemed actors like Tom Hanks and Denzel Washington have experienced. Matthew Perry was no exception to this rule. Despite his rising fame from 'Friends' and the romantic comedy 'Fools Rush In,' he soon discovered the challenges of consistently finding success in the film industry.

Matthew's journey in Hollywood was a testament to the inherent uncertainty of movie-making. Even surrounded by talented actors and acclaimed directors, guaranteeing a film's success was far from straightforward. His burgeoning reputation in the entertainment sphere, bolstered by his television triumphs, offered him opportunities to explore diverse roles in cinema. However, transitioning from a beloved television actor to a film star presented its own set of challenges.

Several of the films Matthew starred in, despite the presence of notable talents both onscreen and off, encountered difficulties in resonating with audiences and critics alike. These projects, falling short in both box office returns and critical reception, highlighted the unpredictable nature of film success. It was a learning curve for Matthew, navigating the complex landscape of Hollywood, where the right combination of story, performance, and audience reception was not always a given. This phase in his career underscored that not every film, regardless of the star power involved, is guaranteed to be a hit.

In 1998, Matthew took on a notable role in the film 'Almost Heroes,' directed by the acclaimed Christopher Guest. The movie cast him as Leslie Edwards, a well-bred aristocrat, alongside the comedic force of Chris Farley, who played a rough-and-tumble character. Their onscreen partnership embarked on a comedic journey, racing against the famed explorers Lewis and Clark to be the first to reach the Pacific Ocean in the early nineteenth century.

Securing the role of Leslie Edwards in 'Almost Heroes' was no small feat for Matthew, as the competition was intense. The part was highly sought after, with Hugh Laurie initially considered a strong contender. However, the film's producers were keen on a more internationally recognized face, given Laurie's then-limited fame outside the United Kingdom. Other renowned actors like Bill Murray and Hugh Grant were also approached but ultimately turned down the role, paving the way for Matthew to step in.

For Matthew, this film was poised to be a dream project. Not only would he be co-starring with Chris Farley, known for his impressive work on 'Saturday Night Live' and 'Tommy Boy,' but he would also be working under the direction of Christopher Guest, famously known as Nigel Tufnel from 'Spinal Tap.' However, the production of 'Almost Heroes' was fraught with challenges. The process involved reshooting and cutting multiple scenes, with many of Matthew's own scenes being reduced to shift the film's focus towards Farley's character.

Filming in the American Heartland during the sweltering heat of summer added to the challenges, with the cast dressed in heavy furs and period costumes. The conditions made the production process particularly gruelling. What should have been an exciting opportunity became a taxing endeavor, further complicated by unforeseen real-life tragedies that cast a shadow over the film's production. This period in Matthew's career was a mix of professional anticipation and the hard realities of filmmaking, illustrating the often-unseen difficulties behind bringing a cinematic vision to life.

On December 18, 1997, the entertainment world was shaken by the tragic news of Chris Farley's death from a drug overdose. This event cast a somber shadow over 'Almost Heroes,' as it turned out to be Farley's final film, released posthumously on May 29, 1998. The film, carrying the weight of this tragedy, struggled at the box office, earning only $6 million against a budget of $30 million. Critics were harsh in their assessments, lamenting that the film did not sufficiently showcase Farley's considerable talents in what became his last cinematic appearance. For Matthew, the film was a mixed experience. While his performance had its moments, it was evident that the studio focused predominantly on Farley, leading to an unbalanced representation that didn't fully utilize Matthew's acting prowess.

In 1999, Matthew starred in 'Three To Tango,' a romantic comedy featuring Neve Campbell and Dylan McDermott. He portrayed Oscar Novak, an architect vying for a significant contract who finds himself entangled in a complicated scenario. Oscar, mistakenly believed to be gay, is hired to spy on a tycoon's mistress, only to find himself falling for her. This storyline resonated with the ongoing joke about Chandler's perceived sexuality in 'Friends,' making the role an interesting choice for Matthew.

However, despite Matthew's enjoyment in working on 'Three To Tango,' the film did not fare well commercially or critically. It only managed to gross half of its $20 million budget. The film drew criticism for relying on dated gay clichés and lacklustre humor, with reviews suggesting that even a standard episode of 'Friends' offered more laughs and less offensive content.

Matthew faced another personal health crisis after the film's release and underwhelming reception. He was hospitalized with a severe case of pancreatitis, an inflammation of the pancreas often linked to drug abuse. This hospitalization underscored the ongoing toll that substance use was taking on his health, a reminder of the challenging path he was navigating amidst his professional endeavors.

Almost Heroes would End Up Being Remembered as the Unfortunate Final Film of Another Comedy Legend

Finally, Another Box Office Hit - But More Trouble Was Present

Matthew Perry's quest for another hit film after 'Fools Rush In' finally saw success in 2000 with the release of the dark comedy 'The Whole Nine Yards.' In this film, he was part of an ensemble cast featuring renowned actors like Bruce Willis, Rosanna Arquette, Michael Clarke Duncan, and Amanda Peet, indicating a promising venture from the start.

In 'The Whole Nine Yards,' Matthew played the character Nicholas 'Oz' Oseransky, a dentist who unexpectedly becomes entangled in a mob ring. The plot unfolds as Oz moves from Canada to Chicago and discovers that his new neighbor is a former hitman on the run from his past in Chicago. This intriguing premise set the stage for a blend of comedy and action.

Contrary to some of his previous cinematic experiences, 'The Whole Nine Yards' emerged as a commercial triumph, garnering more than double its production budget with a gross of $100 million. Not only was it a financial success, but the production environment of the film was markedly more enjoyable than his past projects. The cast had the creative freedom to improvise during filming, allowing Matthew to infuse his scenes with his unique humor, including slapstick comedy and spontaneous jokes. This approach to filming added a dynamic and entertaining element to the movie, contributing to its overall appeal and success.

'The Whole Nine Yards' marked a significant moment in Matthew's film career, demonstrating his versatility and comedic talent in a setting that allowed him more creative expression and interaction with fellow cast members.

But even though he got to showcase more of his comedic chops in this film, the underlying drug issues he had struggled with were becoming too pervasive. The film's production in Montreal, scheduled between the seasons of 'Friends,' coincided with a lifestyle that further complicated his struggles.

Bruce Willis, co-starring in the film and known for his 'Die Hard' fame, played a central role in the off-set dynamics. He rented a penthouse suite in a downtown Montreal hotel, which quickly became the hotspot for the cast's post-shoot gatherings. These parties, often hosted by Willis, were extravagant affairs that stretched into the early morning hours. The allure of these celebrations, fueled by Willis' status as a leading action star and the abundance of alcohol, was irresistible to many, including Matthew.

However, the festive atmosphere of these gatherings contrasted sharply with the challenges Matthew faced each night. Struggling to find sleep after the high-energy parties, he frequently turned to Xanax as a means to wind down. This decision was fraught with risk, especially considering the amount of alcohol he had consumed. The tranquilizer, though effective in bringing him the needed rest, posed a significant danger due to its potentially hazardous interaction with alcohol. Despite being aware of these risks, Matthew felt compelled to use the drug, driven by the need to balance his demanding work schedule with the challenges of his personal life. This period in Matthew's life was a delicate balancing act as he navigated the demands of his burgeoning film career while wrestling with the personal demons of addiction.

He would eventually check into rehab to recover from his Xanax addiction. During this period of recovery and reflection, he found himself watching Julia Roberts on television, accepting her Oscar for 'Erin Brockovich.' Witnessing her triumph was bittersweet; He felt joy for her success but also a sense of personal achievement for having taken steps to confront his addiction. It was a poignant reminder of the dual nature of life in the spotlight — the glamour on one side and personal battles on the other.

However, Matthew's struggles with substance abuse were far from over. A few years later, while working on the 2002 romantic comedy 'Serving Sara,' his battle with addiction resurfaced. In this film, he played a process server who becomes romantically involved with a character portrayed by Elizabeth Hurley. The demands of this project coincided with a period where Matthew was consuming a quart of vodka daily, along with Xanax and other opioids. The severity of his condition led to the postponement of the film's production, as he once again needed to enter rehab for treatment.

The challenges Matthew faced during the filming of 'Serving Sara' were compounded by the film's lackluster performance. Upon its release, it received poor reviews and did not perform well at the box office.

This Film was a Big Hit that Showed Perry's Comedic Talents

Getting Out of Film and Figuring Out What's Next

The journey of 'The Whole Nine Yards' continued with its sequel, 'The Whole Ten Yards,' in 2004, in which Matthew Perry and Bruce Willis reprised their roles. However, despite bringing back many of the original's stars, the sequel couldn't capture the magic of its predecessor. Both financially and critically, the film was a letdown. Its revenue was only a fraction of the original's, and it faced an uphill battle in overcoming harsh critical reviews. The shift in its rating from R to PG-13 also played a part in diluting the edginess and intensity that had contributed to the first film's success.

This experience with 'The Whole Ten Yards' significantly impacted Matthew's outlook on his film career. The disappointment of the sequel and a diminishing interest from studios in casting him for comedic roles led him to reconsider his future in film acting. Despite his immense popularity from 'Friends,' the series' conclusion left him in professional limbo. The end of such a defining chapter in his life left him pondering his next steps as he faced the challenge of reinventing himself in an industry that had changed significantly since his rise to fame.

In response to these challenges, Matthew made a strategic pivot towards dramatic acting, hoping to explore new horizons and redefine his career. This transition led to an opportunity on another television show, though this venture was short-lived. The shift from comedy to drama marked a significant change for Matthew as he sought to navigate the post-'Friends' landscape and carve out a new niche for himself in the acting world.

Not All Films Deserve Sequels

Chapter 6 - His Journey Through Genres

Transitioning from comedy to drama presents a unique set of challenges and opportunities, even for established actors. This shift has been navigated successfully by various actors over the years. For instance, Ed Asner transformed his comedic role in 'The Mary Tyler Moore Show' into a more dramatic character for 'Lou Grant.' Similarly, Bradley Cooper evolved from his comedic roles in 'The Wedding Crashers' and the 'Hangover' series to more serious performances in 'A Star Is Born' and 'American Sniper.'

For Matthew Perry, the transition from comedy to drama represented a crucial turning point in his career. Following the end of 'Friends,' his endeavors in comedic roles were met with limited success, prompting a reassessment of his career path. Fortunately, NBC, his familiar network home, offered him a lifeline with the lead role in a new drama series. One of the entertainment industry's most accomplished screenwriters and playwrights developed this opportunity, presenting a fresh start for Matthew in a different genre.

Additionally, Matthew's personal life was undergoing a significant transformation. Since 2005, he has been actively participating in Alcoholics Anonymous, taking crucial steps toward recovery. Encouraged by his close friend and fellow actor Hank Azaria, Matthew embarked on the challenging journey of the twelve-step program. Matthew's decision to pivot to drama, coupled with his commitment to sobriety, marked an important phase in his life, opening doors to new possibilities and continuing his journey in both his career and personal development.

Following his transition into dramatic acting, 2006 presented a significant opportunity for Matthew Perry with 'Studio 60 on the Sunset Strip,' a new television show created by the esteemed Aaron Sorkin. Sorkin was renowned in the industry, with acclaimed works such as the screenplays for 'A Few Good Men' and 'The American President,' and the creation of the hit series 'The West Wing' and the lesser-known yet impactful 'Sports Night.'

'Studio 60' offered a unique glimpse into the world of television production, focusing on the behind-the-scenes dynamics of a 'Saturday Night Live' style sketch comedy show. In this series, Matthew stepped into the role of Matt Albie, a former writer for the show within the show, who returns to take up the mantle of head writer and producer. The plot revolves around 'Studio 60' grappling with falling ratings and dwindling cultural relevance, with Matt Albie's character critical to revitalizing the show.

Matthew's character in 'Studio 60' mirrored his own professional journey in some ways. Just as Matt Albie was tasked with reinvigorating a struggling show, Matthew was navigating a new phase in his career, seeking to reinvent his persona away from the comedic roles that had defined much of his career. This role in 'Studio 60' was a significant step in Matthew's exploration of dramatic acting, offering him a chance to showcase his versatility and depth as an actor in a project helmed by one of the industry's most respected figures.

Matthew Perry's involvement in 'Studio 60 on the Sunset Strip' saw him sharing the screen with prominent actors, including Bradley Whitford, Amanda Peet, Sarah Paulson, D.L. Hughley, and Nate Corddry. Despite the star-studded cast and receiving critical acclaim, the show faced a brief run, spanning a single season with 22 episodes from 2006 to 2007. One of the critical challenges for 'Studio 60' was its high production costs, which contributed to its untimely conclusion.

Additionally, 'Studio 60' found itself in an accidental rivalry with another NBC show airing around the same time, '30 Rock.' Both shows delved into the world behind a 'Saturday Night Live '-type sketch comedy series, but '30 Rock,' being a comedy, resonated more with audiences and sustained a longer run of seven seasons and over a hundred episodes. In contrast, 'Studio 60,' with its dramatic angle, struggled to secure a similar foothold.

The issue wasn't simply that 'Studio 60' was conceptually similar to '30 Rock.' After all, NBC had successfully aired different genres of shows simultaneously, such as 'Scrubs' and 'ER.' The network had also managed to juggle multiple crime dramas simultaneously. The real challenge for 'Studio 60' lay in its inability to attract a sufficient viewer base to justify its high costs. Perhaps the audience preferred the lighthearted humor of '30 Rock' rather than the more thoughtful drama of 'Studio 60.'

This venture into dramatic television proved more daunting for Matthew than anticipated. While bold and promising, his transition from comedy to drama encountered hurdles that highlighted the unpredictability and challenges of sustaining success in the ever-changing landscape of television entertainment.

Studio 60 was Ambitious but Struggled to Get Ratings

Returning to the Spotlight in Comedy and Beyond

Matthew Perry's return to the comedy genre in 2009 with '17 Again' marked a significant moment in his career trajectory. In this fantastical comedy, he played Mike, a 37-year-old man who experiences a magical transformation back to his 17-year-old self, portrayed by Zac Efron. Although Matthew's performance was integral to the film, it was primarily a platform for Efron, whose popularity had surged following his role as Troy Bolton. This focus helped the film achieve substantial financial success, nearly tripling its budget. Audience reception was generally positive, as reflected in CinemaScore ratings, though it didn't markedly boost Matthew's profile in the industry. Nonetheless, '17 Again' was a pivotal project for him alongside the enduring legacy of 'Friends,' which continued to captivate fans through syndication and DVD collections.

In 2010, Matthew expanded his artistic repertoire by venturing into voice acting with the video game 'Fallout: New Vegas.' Set in a post-apocalyptic world, he voiced Benny, a casino owner and central antagonist. This role in the expansive 'Fallout' universe allowed Matthew to explore new dimensions of character portrayal, further showcasing his versatility as an actor. The player's quest to confront Benny in the desolate ruins of New Vegas added depth to the game's narrative, illustrating Matthew's ability to bring complex characters to life, even in video gaming.

Though not ground-breaking in their scale, these ventures were instrumental in setting the stage for what was to come. With extensive experience in the entertainment industry, Matthew was well-prepared to take on a more influential role in content creation. Driven by a desire for greater creative control and input, he was poised to develop a television show more closely aligned with his vision. This step forward was about career advancement, personal reinvention, and perseverance. As he looked towards this new chapter, Matthew's journey was a testament to his resilience, both professionally and in his ongoing battle with addiction.

As Matthew Perry once reflected, "I've had a life of extreme highs and extreme lows. I've been so blessed with my career, but equally, I've had to face my own inner demons." This sentiment echoes throughout his career transitions, underscoring his resilience and determination. The conclusion of this chapter in Matthew's life story leaves us anticipating his next creative endeavor, a testament to his enduring spirit and his journey toward both personal and professional fulfillment.

At Least Matthew was still Getting the Attention of Audiences in '17 Again'

Chapter 7 - Striving for Sobriety and New Beginnings in Television

Matthew Perry's journey towards sobriety was a challenging road, fraught with personal and professional hurdles. Post-'Friends,' he grappled to find a foothold in the acting world. His stint on 'Studio 60 on the Sunset Strip' was short-lived, lasting only a season. While commercially successful, the film '17 Again' was largely perceived as a Zac Efron vehicle, with Matthew's role not garnering the spotlight he had hoped for. Even his venture into voice acting with 'Fallout: New Vegas' didn't translate into significant recognition, as the game's success wasn't attributed to his participation or that of any specific cast member.

Confronted with these realities, Matthew was at a crossroads. His desire to rediscover his place in the entertainment industry coincided with his battle for sobriety. In a bold move to redefine his career, he decided to take matters into his own hands. This determination led him to venture into a new realm - creating and producing his own television show. In 2009, he embarked on developing a television pilot, a project that would mark his return to the small screen and give him creative control and a fresh platform to showcase his talents.

This new endeavor represented a significant step for Matthew as he sought to leverage his experiences, both triumphant and challenging, into a project that was indeed his own. It was a move that blended his aspirations in the entertainment industry with his personal journey of recovery and growth. As Matthew delved into this ambitious undertaking, it was clear that he was not just seeking a return to TV stardom but also striving to carve out a new path aligned with his evolving artistic vision and personal aspirations.

Perry's venture into creating his own show, 'Mr. Sunshine,' quickly garnered significant attention in the television industry, leading to a competitive bidding war among networks. The show's concept mirrored some aspects of Matthew's life, adding personal relevance to the project. He starred as Ben Donovan, a manager at the modestly sized Sunshine Arena in San Diego. Despite his professional success, Ben, like Matthew, finds himself at a crossroads as he approaches his forties, re-evaluating his life and his choices.

The narrative of 'Mr. Sunshine' resonated with Matthew's real-life experiences. Notable successes had marked his career. Still, his personal battles with substance abuse and the search for a more fulfilling life paralleled Ben's introspective journey. This underlying connection added depth to the show's premise, making it a project close to Matthew's heart.

In late 2009, ABC showed confidence in Matthew's vision by agreeing to produce a pilot for 'Mr. Sunshine.' The deal with ABC featured significant stakes, including substantial penalties if the pilot did not progress to a full series. This agreement underscored the network's commitment to Matthew's concept and belief in its potential success. Working alongside collaborators Marc Firek and Alex Barnow, Matthew devoted 2010 to developing the pilot, culminating in the show's launch as a full series in early 2011.

Assembling the cast for 'Mr. Sunshine' was another crucial step in bringing the show to life. Matthew managed to bring on board notable talents like Allison Janney, who played Ben's boss, and Andrea Anders, portraying a character with a romantic past with Ben. This ensemble of actors added further appeal to the series, combining their diverse talents to create a dynamic and engaging show.

But for Perry, 'Mr. Sunshine', unfortunately, did not culminate in the success he had hoped for. Despite its initial promise and the buzz it generated, the show struggled to maintain its audience. Out of the thirteen episodes produced, only nine were broadcast on television. Just three months following its debut, 'Mr. Sunshine' was canceled, and the unaired episodes found a home only on the official DVD release of the series. The viewership ratings saw a significant decline, with the final episode attracting merely half the audience of the premiere, reflecting the show's inability to sustain viewer interest over its course.

Amidst the show's struggles, Matthew faced personal challenges of his own. He announced his return to rehab in a statement that, while brief, incorporated a touch of his characteristic humor. True to his Chandler Bing persona, Matthew quipped about the situation, remarking that people were free to resume making jokes about him behind his back. This blend of candor and wit was reminiscent of the style he brought to his 'Friends' character, where humor often served as a coping mechanism during difficult times.

The cancellation of 'Mr. Sunshine' and Matthew's return to rehab were setbacks in his quest for a post-'Friends' resurgence in the television landscape. The show's failure to resonate with audiences and his ongoing personal struggles marked a challenging phase in his career. Yet, Matthew's ability to maintain his sense of humor, even in adversity, indicated the resilience and perseverance that had characterized his journey in the entertainment industry. As Chandler Bing might have quipped in a similar situation, "Could this be any more challenging?" This approach to life's hurdles, blending humor with realism, continued to be a defining trait of Matthew Perry's persona, both on and off the screen.

Mr. Sunshine was a Big Show for ABC

From 'Mr. Sunshine' to 'Go On': Matthew's Quest for a Hit Show

Matthew Perry's determination to succeed in television remained unshaken by the cancellation of 'Mr. Sunshine.' With an unwavering resolve, he embarked on a new project with NBC a year later, when he created 'Go On.' Once again taking on the dual role of star and producer, Matthew enlisted the expertise of Scott Silveri, a former colleague from his 'Friends' days. Silveri, who had risen through the ranks on 'Friends' from story editor to executive producer and had also contributed to 'Joey,' the spin-off starring Matt LeBlanc, brought valuable experience to the new endeavor.

In 'Go On,' Matthew portrayed Ryan King, a sports talk radio host grappling with the loss of his wife. The narrative followed his journey of grief and healing as he joined a support group, meeting others facing their own personal challenges. The show boasted a dynamic ensemble cast, including Laura Benanti, Tyler James Williams, John Cho, Allison Miller, and Piper Perabo. It even featured cameos by former professional football star Terrell Owens.

Despite its promising premise and a cast that sparkled with talent, 'Go On' struggled to capture a substantial audience. Even with a coveted time slot following the popular show 'The Voice,' it languished at the bottom of the ratings and was ultimately canceled after its 22-episode run. This setback, however, did not mark the end of Matthew's television endeavors.

Matthew found another opportunity in dramatic television with his role in the critically acclaimed CBS series 'The Good Wife.' Appearing in four episodes between 2012 and 2013, he portrayed Mike Kresteva, an attorney vying for the Illinois governorship. His performance was well-received, leading to him reprising the role in 'The Good Fight,' a spin-off of 'The Good Wife,' for three episodes. These appearances in high-profile dramas showcased Matthew's versatility and ability to seamlessly transition between comedy and drama, reaffirming his status as a talented actor capable of adapting to diverse roles.

A Last Shot At TV

A blend of creative involvement and personal challenges marked Matthew Perry's final foray into television. In 2015, he took on a triple role as creator, star, and executive producer in a new adaptation of 'The Odd Couple' for CBS. This sitcom, rooted in Neil Simon's classic play, had seen earlier transformations into film and television. Matthew had harbored ambitions to revive this story for some time, but studios had repeatedly overlooked his proposals. Despite this and the time spent on 'Go On,' he remained convinced of the potential of his passion project.

Finally, in 2013, CBS recognized the promise in Matthew's vision and greenlit a pilot. The show debuted in 2015 as a mid-season replacement, introducing a fresh take on the iconic story. In this latest iteration, Matthew portrayed Oscar Madison, a carefree slob, opposite Thomas Lennon's Felix Unger, a meticulous and orderly character. The series focused on the comedic dynamics between Oscar, a sports talk radio host, and Felix, a photographer and yoga instructor, as they navigated their contrasting lifestyles and searched for love.

The reimagined 'The Odd Couple' sought to capture the timeless humor of the original while offering a contemporary twist, with Matthew infusing his personal touch into the character of Oscar. The show was a significant undertaking for him, representing another acting role and a deeper involvement in the creative process. The project combined his comedic talent with his aspirations as a creator and producer, reflecting his evolution in the entertainment industry.

Despite mixed critical reception, 'The Odd Couple' found a fanbase that appreciated the dynamic between Matthew Perry and Thomas Lennon. Their onscreen chemistry resonated with viewers, earning Matthew two People's Choice Award nominations. The show's run, encompassing three seasons and 38 episodes, was a testament to its appeal among audiences. Matthew addressed the show's cancellation with his characteristic humor and resilience, jokingly noting the sudden nature of the show's end as if the production room's door had been painted over without his knowledge.

Following 'The Odd Couple,' Matthew entered a different television format with the 2017 miniseries 'The Kennedys: After Camelot.' This project departed from the mainstream networks Matthew had previously worked with, as it aired on Reelz, a less prominent cable network. Despite this shift, the series boasted a strong cast and delved into the compelling narrative of the Kennedy family in the aftermath of Robert Kennedy's assassination in 1968.

Matthew took on the role of Senator Ted Kennedy, showcasing his ability to embody a complex historical figure. The cast included Katie Holmes as Jacqueline Kennedy Onassis, Diana Hardcastle as Rose Kennedy, Alexander Siddig as Aristotle Onassis, Barry Pepper as Robert Kennedy, and Tom Wilkinson as

Joseph P. Kennedy Sr. The series received favorable reviews for portraying the Kennedy family's trials and tribulations, although its viewership numbers reflected the challenges of being on a lesser-known network. Each part of the miniseries attracted about three-quarters of a million viewers, indicative of Reelz's limited reach and recognition among television audiences.

These two projects highlighted Matthew's versatility as an actor and his willingness to explore diverse roles and platforms. From the lighthearted sitcom environment of 'The Odd Couple' to the historical drama of 'The Kennedys: After Camelot,' Matthew demonstrated his commitment to his craft. Despite the varying degrees of success, these ventures were crucial in Matthew's ongoing journey in the entertainment industry as he navigated new challenges and continued to leave his mark as a talented and adaptable actor.

The Trailer for The Odd Couple Shows How Enduring the Story Is

Chapter 8 - The End of a Life

The inevitable conclusion of life's journey is a reality for all, and for Matthew Perry, this end came far sooner than anticipated. Following the conclusion of 'The Odd Couple' in 2017, Matthew found himself in professional limbo, struggling to secure new roles. However, the more daunting challenge he faced was not in his career but in his health, which was rapidly deteriorating.

In a harrowing turn of events in 2018, Matthew's health took a critical hit when he fell into a coma after his colon burst, a severe complication stemming from his long-standing opioid usage. The damage inflicted on his colon led to catastrophic gastrointestinal issues, necessitating an emergency surgery that spanned an arduous seven hours. The situation was dire; Matthew remained in a coma for two weeks and subsequently spent nearly five months in the hospital. During this critical period, he was reliant on life support, and his chances of recovery hung precariously in the balance.

Defying the slim odds of survival, Matthew exhibited remarkable resilience. After enduring fourteen surgeries and the challenges of being on life support, he emerged from the hospital. His recovery journey included the use of a colostomy bag for nine months, a humbling and challenging experience he faced with both embarrassment and acceptance.

This phase of Matthew's life was a testament to his physical strength and highlighted his mental and emotional fortitude. Despite the overwhelming odds and the stigma associated with his condition, Matthew persevered, displaying an admirable spirit of survival.

Continuing Struggles and Revelations

Despite his significant earnings from 'Friends,' where he made $1 million per episode, Matthew Perry's wealth was heavily invested in his arduous battle for sobriety. In his candid autobiography, 'Friends, Lovers, and the Big Terrible Thing,' released in 2022, Matthew revealed the extent of his struggles with addiction. He shockingly disclosed that he had been to rehab at least fifteen times, with numerous additional stints kept away from public knowledge. His efforts to attain sobriety were not only emotionally taxing but also financially draining, with an estimated $7 million spent in pursuit of recovery.

This staggering sum, equivalent to his earnings from seven episodes of 'Friends' at the height of his career, underscored the profound impact of his addiction. He recounted a particularly challenging time during the production of 'Serving Sara,' where he shouldered over half a million dollars. This amount covered the costs incurred from halting production and subsequent post-production efforts, including re-recording dialogue. Despite his attempts to promote the film and rectify the situation, it ultimately failed to resonate commercially or critically.

In another revelation from his book, Matthew shared a missed opportunity in the film industry. He was initially cast in a journalistic role alongside Meryl Streep in Adam McKay's 2020 film 'Don't Look Up.' However, his ongoing health issues and a rehab stint, compounded by a life-threatening incident involving CPR for a stopped heart, led to his withdrawal from the project.

Matthew's personal life, particularly his romantic relationships, also faced challenges. He was engaged to Molly Hurwitz, a literary agency manager, from 2018 to 2021, with the engagement announced in late 2020. However, the relationship ended a few months later. Outside of his brief romance with Julia Roberts and a fleeting moment with Valerie Bertinelli, Matthew's love life remained relatively low-profile.

In his book, Matthew expressed a deep-seated fear of 'the big terrible thing,' a reference to the possibility of living with a colostomy bag permanently. This fear encapsulated the physical and emotional toll of his health battles, symbolizing the ongoing challenges he faced in his journey toward recovery and well-being. His autobiography thus painted a picture of a man grappling with the weight of fame, health issues, and the pursuit of personal happiness, offering a raw and honest look into the life of a beloved television star.

The Final Curtain: 'Friends: The Reunion'

In 2021, Matthew Perry returned to the screen for one last memorable appearance, this time for a special event that tugged at the heartstrings of 'Friends' fans worldwide. 'Friends: The Reunion,' streamed on HBO Max, brought together Matthew and the rest of the iconic cast for a nostalgic journey back to some of the most cherished sets of the show. This reunion celebrated the series that had defined a generation, providing a rare opportunity for the cast to reminisce about their experiences and the impact 'Friends' had on their lives and careers.

The reunion was not just a trip down memory lane for the cast; it also featured many guests who shared their connections and memories related to the show. From Lady Gaga donning a show-themed costume to Cindy Crawford and members of the global sensation BTS, who spoke about how 'Friends' aided them in learning English, the special was a testament to the show's far-reaching influence.

During the reunion, fans noticed Matthew's slightly swollen appearance, which his representatives attributed to his recent dental surgery before the filming. Despite this, Matthew's presence at the reunion was a poignant reminder of his enduring bond with his fellow cast members and the timeless appeal of 'Friends.' The special was a fitting tribute to the show's legacy, allowing fans and the cast alike to revisit the magic that made 'Friends' a cultural phenomenon.

For Matthew, 'Friends: The Reunion' represented more than just a reunion; it was a celebration of a pivotal chapter in his life and career, a chapter filled with laughter, camaraderie, and unforgettable moments. As the cast gathered to relive the show's glory, it was a bittersweet reminder of the journey they had shared, a journey that had brought them together as a family both on and off the screen.

Matthew Perry: A Life Remembered

The journey of Matthew Perry, a beloved figure in television and film, came to a tragic conclusion on October 28, 2023. At the age of 54, Perry was found unresponsive in his Los Angeles home, specifically in his hot tub. The circumstances surrounding his untimely passing remain unclear, but authorities confirmed that there was no indication of foul play, and no drugs were found on the property.

In the wake of his passing, a private funeral service was held, attended by his closest companions, including all five of his castmates from 'Friends.' This gathering of friends and family was a testament to Matthew's impact on the lives of those around him. The service was not just a farewell but also a celebration of a life that, while marked by challenges, was filled with laughter, talent, and memorable moments that touched the hearts of millions.

Matthew Perry's final resting place is at the Forest Lawn Memorial Park in the Hollywood Hills. Laid to rest in the Sanctuary of Love outdoor mausoleum section, he is in the company of other notable figures such as Debbie Reynolds, Carrie Fisher, Andy Gibb, and Michael Clarke Duncan. This section of the memorial park, known for its serenity and beauty, offers a fitting and peaceful final abode for someone who brought so much joy and entertainment to others.

His legacy, defined by his iconic role as Chandler Bing and various other contributions to the entertainment industry, continues to live on. Through his performances, Matthew Perry brought laughter and relatability to his audience, creating a lasting imprint on popular culture. Though marked by personal struggles, his life is a reminder of the resilience and strength inherent in the human spirit. Matthew Perry's story, with its highs and lows, will remain an integral part of Hollywood's rich tapestry, remembered and celebrated by fans and colleagues alike.

A Final Word

The life of Matthew Perry, though cut short, was marked by remarkable resilience, relentless passion, and an undying commitment to bringing joy to others. His story is not just one of a celebrated actor who captivated millions as Chandler Bing in 'Friends,' but of a man whose life was a tapestry of triumphs, challenges, and a relentless pursuit of happiness. Perry's journey through the entertainment world showcased his versatile talent and innate ability to connect with audiences through humor and authenticity.

Matthew's struggles with addiction, a battle he fought bravely throughout his life, paint a picture of a man who, despite personal hardships, never lost sight of his love for the craft. His dedication to his profession, his tenacity in the face of adversity, and his remarkable sense of humor are the qualities that endeared him to fans and colleagues alike. He was more than just a phenomenal actor; he was a beacon of perseverance, constantly striving to overcome obstacles and make the most of his talents.

Perry's legacy extends beyond his roles on screen. He was a man who understood the power of laughter, the importance of determination, and the necessity of facing life's challenges head-on. His story is a poignant reminder of the human struggle with addiction and the importance of seeking help. It serves as an inspiration for anyone battling personal demons, underscoring the need to prioritize mental and physical health.

Though marred by personal struggles, Matthew's life was also filled with moments of joy and achievements that continue to resonate. He brought laughter and light into the lives of many, a testament to his character and impact on entertainment. His portrayal of Chandler Bing will forever be cherished. Still, Matthew Perry's true legacy lies in how he touched lives — through his art, resilience, and humanity.

In the words of Chandler Bing, "It's a small world, and somehow, I never run into Beyonce." This humorous reflection captures the essence of Perry's ability to find humor even in the most ordinary moments. This blend of wit, charm, and relatability will keep Matthew Perry's memory alive in the hearts of his fans and friends. As we remember him, we celebrate not just the actor but the man who, despite life's challenges, brought a unique brightness to our world.

Final Surprise Bonus

Hope you've enjoyed this biography of Matthew Perry.

We always like to give more than we get, so I'd like to give you one final bonus.

Do me a favor, if you enjoyed this book, please leave a review on Amazon.

It'll help get the word out so more kids can find out more about Matthew Perry!

If you do, I'll send you one of my most cherished video collection – Free:

Ultimate Collection of Links to Matthew Perry's YouTube Videos!

You won't be able to say you know Matthew Perry until you watch these videos!

Here's how to claim your free videos:

1. Leave a review right away -

2. Send a screenshot of your review to:
reviews@allaboutbookseries.com with the subject line:
Matthew Perry the Undisclosed Biography Review

3. Receive your free video collection – *"Ultimate Collection of Links to Matthew Perry's YouTube Videos!"* – immediately!

Made in the USA
Las Vegas, NV
09 February 2024

85523230R00052